SHROUDED SKIES

by

KAP 5

Shrouded Skies

ISBN: 978-1-0692300-0-3

Published by False 9 Publishing © 2024

Author's Note

This is my contribution to the world.
I have been writing for as long as I can remember, maybe since I was 7. And for all these years, I have kept on writing as I went to school, then high school, then college, and now while working full time. I have been unbelievably busy with work these last couple of years, putting off publishing my works, and most of my interests for that matter. Well, life gets busy, and if you can't make time for yourself and for people and things you care for, living loses its worth. This is the life my works belong to, and they shall get it. Even when all of this was compiled together invading late nights, in a haste.

The poems here are an interesting study of my world-view just as they are an interesting study of the world itself. The poems in this book were written roughly between the ages of 12 and 25. Most of them are my thoughts and some of them are fictional rhymes. I hope you find something you connect with.

More to come!

મમ્મી અને પપ્પા, તમારા માટે...

Table of Contents

Youth

Mid-age

Old-age

KAP 5

It is the battlecry, beautiful and fierce,
It is the titanic light, sharp and alarming;
The thunder and its lightning will pierce
All, with shooting rain, as it descends down storming.

KAP 5

What Now?

When you've put it all on the line
And then you find yourself on cloud nine
The heights scaled and the treasures of the deep you plough,
For all of it to be met with the question, "What now?"

For the sweat that it soaked and then demanded some more
For the strength it took till your willpower was sore
And when you step on the podium facing the awestruck world and bow
A fleeting thought emerges, asking "What now?"

Danced with fate and battled with the stars
Fell down and then got back up again powered by your scars
And the world singing to you with all the noise your ears could allow

And then it lets in a faint whisper inquiring
"What now?"

There is only the path and the path alone, no
such thing as obstacles
Make your way forward, unbothered,
performing spectacles,
And that is what you do, remember, as your
conquests will endow
You with the question at the finish line, "What
now?"

Serenade

Bamboozled poets have serenaded the moon of their skies
For a long year, from whence every speck of their beauty lies.
Gazing deep, hypnotized, they call themselves bravehearts,
Crossing dimensions in that infamous emotion, which is, in equal parts
Selfish and selfless, strength and weakness, faith and doubt.
Long have these crazed poets run their pens out
Fathoming an eternal state of unsaturated amalgamation
As the fated fools can't be separated since their creation
As fantasies are translated into gibberish realities
Of pixelated proportions and colossal calamities

As they fold and collapse onto themselves without a clatter
Or so it seems from the outside, but that view apparently doesn't matter -
As the serenade still rings, from above and beneath,
As they weave fantasies to attain, but not live with.

Gold

You do not need to have an eye for gold.
Chuck away everything that's obsolete because
it's old,
Add one more gadget to your studded throne
In the dilapidated hut you call home,
It doesn't have to be this way
You saw it through, you say;
Rub the scaly rock on the glass screen
To polish it, to make it clean,
Holograms of tangible visions
Lucid from repetitive revisions,
Away from the blunt ground
Where everything sharp is found.
Avoiding copper's sting
Because gold is always king.

You boast the advice that you regurgitated
After severing the tie from where it originated
And you've discreetly paid off the bill
Managing to be unbothered still.

A step is a mountain

And a dew drop is a fountain
And there's lightyears within reach
When you say you've nailed the tide to the beach.
And it's been long since you found vantage actually cumbers,
And of course the disillusioned come in numbers;
You often wake yourself up from sound sleep at night
From that sudden sink, a fall that feels all too real in its own right,
But what does it matter when you are the one who defines
Everything that goes on your throne is golden because it shines.

Fighting Against The Tide

Fighting against the tide
With a shadow by your side
And unheard stories in a language that's
extinct.
One against all, just the wolf and its instinct,
And a world forever spinning.

And somewhere, further up the road
Is a clone fighting, following the same code,
The same map, leading to the same destination,
And you're not the only one taken by the
manifestation
Of breaking out and winning.

Strokes after strokes, and steps after steps
New places while going around the same old
laps,
And the closer you get, the further it seems -
The mirage will go away when the sun dims.
And when it does, you're all alone again.
So you sell and sell, making fools,

Making the world finally play by your rules.
A lone wolf, and a whole herd of sheep,
And no code for you to keep,
No order for you to understand.

Taken by the pursuit, now a second nature to you,
Everything's a stepping-stone, every tick's a cue,
As you begin losing words from the only language you spoke
Trying to satisfy a hunger that can never be stoked
As you don't recognize it anymore.

But what does it matter for all the bridges already burnt
When all you want is to catch the current.

Hey, Look! That's The Master Of The World!

"Mother, I gotta go,
Got myself an early morning tomorrow,
Every night I count on my finger tips
The hours I'll snore in my sleep.
Mother, I gotta go,
I'll call you tomorrow.'

Every morning we run,
Chasing something we loathe,
Giving it stolen time.
No time left to feed our passion.

Living on the run
With a bag of chips –
And the damages that we incur
With loads of sugar
In everything we eat.

Can't start a day without big cups of coffee,
Having bloodshot eyes with the lack of sleep,

High on caffeine that you can't even blink
So tired that you don't have the power to think.
"Hey, look! That's the Master of the World!"

Every morning we run
Chasing something we loathe,
Giving it stolen time.
No time left to feed our passion.

So engrossed in something
That matters so little to you;
Reminiscing those times when you really used to dream;
You had dreams, at least a few...
Do not pretend you did not use to dream.
Deep inside, that's the only thing that keeps you going,
Flowing like a stream
With no origin –
Flowing crushed between hard rocks
No time or space for docks.
At nights you get calm,
And run manically when the dawn arrives.
Only you can tell how it thrives.

With waters stolen from fresh brooks,
It runs from the dreamlands
To the polluted city.
Still thinking it is pretty.
With no regards and so much haste that you flee,
Will you ever meet the sea?
The sea that you like?

"Hey, look! That's the Master of the World!"

Oh, Bird

Oh, unsure bird, are you stoked?
Or has your conscience been revoked?
You lie there, when outside it's cold
And lament all your dreams have been sold.

Oh, lost bird, remember back when you used to sing?
Back when you hadn't been burdened by a heavy wing.
Why'd you feel you've failed every plan?
Looking for something that's right in your wingspan.

Oh, cynical bird, why don't you look out?
It's summer again and the sun's out and about.
Are you waiting for when the thunder rumbles?
And witness again how your nest crumbles?

Oh, mighty bird, do not climb me up the table
Even though it goes with the script of a perfect fable.

Oh, wounded bird, after your longing yelp
How is the worst thing anyone can do is help?

Oh, lonely bird, do not turn into stone,
We'll always fly together, even if you want to fly this alone.

Generations

Let's set the scene, the buck has been passed
It has been said, it has been signed.
And it is the talk, we have been outclassed
Or so has the truth been aligned.
We can't race time, and that is our sin
Competing against a head start, we fell short
And there it all goes in the bin
As we are forced to abort
The worlds we build, for us to live in
And the songs we write:
As they tell us what to believe in
And whatever we say, we're never right.
And we shouldn't be surprised
We speak different tongues
Share the same words, but never realized
The voice comes out different from our lungs;
And we have been taught
And we have been raised
Where wisdom can't be bought
And the wise can't be praised;
We go building our own worlds away
This is what we were made to do:
Not to repeat what we were taught to say

Didn't we want to start anew?
We will, as they did,
And will be once in the same place
Sowing the same seed
Claiming our head start in a made-up race.

Lone Cloud

And the world will go to sleep
Leaving you in the wake
Of certainties you had to keep
And the deadlines you had to make
While the candle burns away.

And you will be left wandering
And looking at that lone cloud
In the blue sky, quietly laundering
The untranslatable thoughts so loud
Which are here to stay.

Test of fire, dipping in the deep end
With the world on your back,
Swimming to no avail in search of land
With water up to your neck
With comfort at bay.

And in the darkness, you found your home
Chipping away at the night
Quietly, as you are awake by your own

In search of the elusive light
Which only appears at day.

And you knew the mirror lies
And you still choose to believe
And watch in silence as a part of you dies
While the rest of you elects to live
And while you have worked alone
You have longed for company
While you have strained your heart, muscle and bone
You have longed for symphony
A symphony for the road
A symphony for the flow
As what soothes your abode
Is watching something grow
As you find pieces long lost
With the candle of hope
Which has burned into the day with a cost
Inferior to the treasure that had eloped
And while you know there aren't just a few
You light up other candles
With the light now inside of you.
And with the light you lovingly dandle

The dark world,
Come what may, come what may.

Somewhere

Afternoon, aftertaste of the sour tang of orange juice
But there's the sweetness as well; well, somewhere.
Midnight, midway through the dance, we introduce
Ourselves, but there's familiarity as well; well, from somewhere.

You looked into my eyes and I was lost
And I see you were too.
Mourning our own low tides, at what cost?
Drenched in the old, pretending we wanted something new.

Let me take emotion for a spin
Let us see if we can still feel something.
At least we can hurt, we don't have to come clean,
We don't have to say a word, we don't have to promise anything.

Yesterday, yesteryears of unreliable memories
But there's the sweetness as well; well,
somewhere.
Tonight, tomorrows of uncertain waiting
tragedies
But there's familiarity as well; well, from
somewhere.

Little Perfect Utopia

Calm lights resting, watching over the snow on the pavements;
Crisp air, lonely street, watched over by the moon above.
Little perfect paradise, little perfect utopia
But sadly it's only human to yearn for more –
Blinking lights, impatient, watching over the traffic on the overcrowded roads;
Dodge eye-contact from a clone with a broken back
Retiring back to their abode; leaving again before it is healed.
Looking at little perfect paradises, little perfect utopias through squinted eyes
At night;
Yawn away because sadly it's only utopia – a fantasy –
A fantasy that would sizzle in friction with the reality outside the walls.
But sadly, it's only human to yearn for more –

Even though it means straying away from paradise,
Sometimes that's all it means.
Squinting eyes, drowned in sleep, thinking of a rhyme only at night
And thinking there's always tomorrow, and there always will be, each day.

But one night when the rhyme will come to a tired mind,
The broken back will heal, and reminiscing, a smile will emerge.
Quaint lights, serene, smiling back, watching over
The little perfect paradise, the little perfect utopia -
And gladly, it's only human to yearn for more.

It's Too Late In The Night For Love

Clocks froze when we touched
And the world kept us safe in its womb.
And we loved and we had so much
Of our jewels that are now buried in a tomb.
Crossed multiples and possibilities
From space and time and we still wondered
How could that be a reality engraved in our
tame abilities.
And we found out why when we suffered.
Don't let them fool you for your sake -
They will always have a voice to sing the songs
of love
And the same despairing voice to sing the songs
of heartbreak.
So, let fate rain from up above,
Let the stars fall and suns set
Let the memories fall somewhere
Between nostalgia and regret.
Because neither you nor me, if we're being fair,
Like this feeling of trying to fill something
empty

And somehow end up taking more out of it, but
you see,
We should've known as we've danced this dance
before, you and me
And our feet trace the same disasters
Bittersweet.

And the hourglass is frozen
Somewhere between contempt and exhaustion
And the flags have been risen
But we're blind to the caution –
Two magicians, awestruck
As the spells do not work anymore;
Two dreamers stuck
As they don't really sleep at all.
But when the moon arrives
For its exquisite show every night
World retches us out of its womb where our
love thrives
And we crumble like sand in the hourglass
falling with all its might.
We see each other and we see reflections
Of our scars and choices,
As we finish portraits of our affections

Dictated by lost voices.
And we sigh and we try to get back to our sheltered cove,
But baby, it's too late in the night for love...

When

When the prayers ring to return to normalcy
And the startled heart fears dormancy
Waiting in line outside oblivion's gate,
Feeling ambitious in a nestled stalemate.

When the unheard voices render the throat sore
And eyes feel sleepy with all the weight they bore,
And the body and mind find themselves in a disconnect
And the heart is left stranded with no time to react.

When the feet detour from the steps
Going around on eggshells on a million laps
Finding them headed back to oblivion's gate,
Wondering if this really is their fate.

And the rain will fall from the raging clouds
Ridding the azure skies of their shrouds

And the gift from the heavens will come down
for you
Enriching, with petrichor and the morning dew.

Death By Variety

Under the influence of tame emotions,
Tongue-tied, in disbelief, in lingual sobriety,
With a storm of thoughts of colossal proportions
You experience a death by variety.

Assault on the senses, unbiased, on all fronts,
Eat, drink, watch, play, listen, buy, do - dictated by dispersed propriety,
In ten numbers, twenty-six letters, twenty four hours, twelve months,
You experience a death by variety.

Straight as an arrow, with fingers in a number of pies
Because a safety net for a safety net is not enough in its entirety,
Occupied between home and the road, past and the future, truth and lies,
You experience a death by variety.

Sleepless at a random time, irrespective of day or night,
Get lost in a rabbithole of introspection about what we call society,
Between blank faces, monotonicity, and a blinding white light,
You experience a death by variety.

Go, Go

Go, go, your time starts now,
Go to your cottage in the woods,
Or that farmhouse you bought
Haggling with someone just as tired as you,
Go, go!

Go, go,
The time will be up soon,
Go, go!

Go, go,
See the zoo,
Or visit a monastery in Kathmandu,
Fill up the gas in your car,
Go further than far,
Keep driving or make a stop,
But be back before your time is up.
Go, go!

Go, go!

Pack up a fancy bag,

Head towards a camp,
Take the violin classes that you've always
wanted to,
But you won't be satisfied,
Because your time will be up.
So,
Go, go!

Go, go!

Go visit your awkwardly funny grandma,
Go on a date with your soulmate to Taj Mahal in
India,
Or go see the salt flats of Bolivia.
Go to that tiny place where you've always
wanted to grab a bite,
Catch a movie or two on a Friday night,
Experience El Clásico at the Camp Nou,
Or go wherever you wanna go.
Before your time is up,
Go, go!

Hurry up!!

Go, go!

Go, go,
Go far beyond your reach,
Go basking on a beach,
But don't forget your expensive sunglasses on the beach chair,
As you race back home
When the time is up.
Now, go, go!

When you reach home,
You're tired,
You realize,
Time went away rather quickly...
I told you so.
I told you, "Go, go!"

Wake up to the infernal alarm
Set on the blazingly bright screen of your phone.
Go back to the monotonous life,
To listen someone bark at you;
Don't blame them, they're just as tired as you.

Go home to find just the time to sleep.
As you snore, you forget the promises you had to keep,
The promises you made when you were gone.
The morning will come soon,
So,
Go, go!
Go to sleep,
Go, go!

It's morning, go do it all over again,
Do it all over again
Until it's time to really
Go, go!

Wake up, and go, go!!

There's Fireworks In The Sky

There's fireworks in the sky
And we're old and we breathe in the cold air
Under the clouds, and the moon's too shy
To come out, as we sit in our chairs
On the rooftop. Among their innocent laughter
Time slows down.
Forget worrying what comes after
And we forget how to frown.
And that's the smell of mum's stew!
Elated, we race down the stairs,
We were not tired from all the kites we flew,
There was no doubt anywhere...

That was the time
When we would go to our mothers
With scraped knees
And a dirty tee
Falling off a bicycle
That was too big for ourselves -
And we wouldn't care
And we wouldn't care

Because we were ready to take on the world.
And those were the days
When we would just sit and stare at the sky
Just stare at the sky
When the moon is showing off its scars
And we know one night
We'd count all the stars.
'Cause we'll all be together
Even though it's not a promise to keep.
On the roof, we'd bring beds and pillows
Even though we don't intend to sleep;
We'd laugh and cry our hearts out
As the moon and stars eavesdrop.
And slowly the sun will come out
Otherwise we know we'd never stop.
And even though it's not a promise to keep,
We do.

Aspirations

It's a rush, preparing for a test
When the proximity is promising a possibility of perfection.
It's a delicate unrest
Of those butterflies in the stomach
When the reality of dreams becomes more than a fantasy.
It's a world assisted by flawless luck
When creativity becomes the architecture of potency.
It's the little green book in the red box with pictures
Cut and drawn - blueprints of an imperial elegance.
It's the sparkle in the eyes each morning
Welcoming what the dawn has giftwrapped.
It's the loss of rhyme but the prevalence of meaning:
Aspirations of hopping carefreely in the cobbled streets of a city.

Washed away the rage, drowned down the cries -
The smell, the sound and the view settles;
Tired, bearing the burdens of shrouded skies
With gentle crackling, the rain rattles.

Yet

Yet we still believe, that something handbuilt
Will outlive something woven by nature.
And yet we hope for a mountain made of silt
And an underdog taking the fight beyond
stature.
Take a piece of the common cake
And long for a vicarious sweetness,
And yet we continue to put everything at stake
And then mark it obsolete and useless.
Afraid to inadvertently direct
We give up helping it shape
And yet we choose to proudly stand erect
Washing hands off of the resultant state.
And our feet now tread
Where we don't need brakes.
And now we are led
To places with empty mistakes -
Still we live like it's our last day
And pretend we don't need help.
Leaving blank wills and with nothing to say
With mouths so full of ourselves.

New Devices

They got their convincing new devices
Replacing the obsolete ones they tossed:
When they invent perpetual happiness and paradises
Will we stand there with our arms crossed?
Arms crossed, with an incurable itch
And a sweat with a hint of anxiety;
Didn't buy in in the lottery that made everyone rich
In this, are we allowed to call, 'society'?
In the bubble on our best behaviour
Rejected the tactile heavens for a cloudy day.
Applications closed for the position of our saviour,
We'll look for new gods to pray.
We intake bribed pride in staying true
While everybody is changing colours to fit in.
The black sheep, more of a lone wolf
On the road not taken, critiquing.
Go against everything we stand for
Just to stay true to our word;

Bitter, under our breath we abhor
When the milk has already spilled to curd.
Holding onto majestic dark clouds,
Kicking the ground further down below,
When the time comes to sew our shrouds
Will we have reaped what we currently sow?

On The Highway During Dinner Time

On the highway during dinner time
Chasing dim lights under the moon's lime,
In little time it has become
Second nature, which we're yet to overcome –
Tranquil sights, flaunting, welcoming
Desperately a look oncoming,
A look poised onto mirrors which
Don't reflect, rather just show the looker a glitch
Which is fulfilling, yet empty.

The waters, circumnavigated stretches never seen
Witness to the creation and destruction alike of all things that have ever been –
Vessels of hopes and dreams, stories and history,
Touched the feet of those who died chasing glory;
So fierce, yet so serene, calming, guiding

Heard so many wails, and secrets from those
who found it worth confiding,
And sent them around the world, without
spilling,
Reflecting perfect and real images, although
sometimes not fulfilling
But always trustworthy.

Triple Point

You measure it with all the different gauges
Twinning beyond common oddities
And yet you measure it again at different stages
Reduced to singular possibilities
Of a circle drawn on paper:
Ice, water and vapour
But all the same at the core.

You say it in a million languages
Still no one can comprehend,
You use all known phrases
Falling short of the word 'understand'
As you draw a helpless gaze
Reciprocating the one you've always
Seen with eyes this sore.

You see it in every possible light
Mirage of tactile probabilities
You go with the judgement of the sight
And all its tame capabilities;
Translating energies into fickle visions

Poorly read through countless revisions
Making sure that the seed of doubt stays.

You do it in all the ways
With the meaning of 'right' switching.
You turn nights into days
Trapped in the insolent glitching
Of ice, water, vapour; sun, moon, stars -
Coexisting in a single multiple of scarce -
Overlapping gauges, languages, visions and
ways.

Broken Clock

Submitting to the broken clock
Governing with hollow deadlines -
Answering to that empty knock
Of an entity come to collect fines.
Calibrating with mistaken milestones
That are few and far between,
Imitating holograms like clones,
Which are yet to be seen.

Weighing worth on a faulty scale
Measured by non-uniform units -
Building conscience with thoughts left stale
Making do with whatever fits.
Upholding illegible books
Teaching how to read but not write,
Fooled by the cover's looks
Then overwhelmed by the pen's might.

Blank Books

I think I see a thousand people everyday
With a thousand stories
That they do not have the time to tell.

I think I see many familiar faces
With some connections
But none of them ring a bell.

I think I see us
So hollow from the inside
Regurgitating hypocrisy.

I think I see us
Marching into oblivion
Accepting all the futility.

Do you think,
Oh, do you think?
Do you think
He just sits there and laughs
Seeing us running amuck?

Do you think,
Oh, do you think?
Do you think
He feels pity yet enjoys
Watching us struggle in the ruck?

I see blank books nobody has time to write.

I think I see
People giving up on their stories
And accepting a small part in someone else's.

I think I see
People in bandwagons
Blindly believing what they know are fallacies.

I think I see us
Getting into an argument
Over something that matters to none.

I think I see us
Bond over something,
Something that's mutually fun.

Do you think,
Oh, do you think?
Do you think
He who made these rules
Cracks up on how monotonously we live by them?

Do you think,
Oh, do you think?
Do you think
He secretly roots for the black sheep
Who has figured out His scam?

All I see are blank books nobody has time to write.

Still

With all the daylight wasted on lamented dormancies
And the subtle taunts in the scattered discrepancies
That run aplenty; the heaviness that nails the heart to the ground
Soars high, pitching a mirage of unbothered properties staying sound.
And once again, we are hypnotised or deceived, or something of its likeness
As we yet again console ourselves noticing the beauty in stillness;
And it is a tricky plane, for sometimes, it is the final place
And as we now know everything goes around in circles with unforgiving grace -
It could be the start too, this stillness, and it will always leave a doubt:
For it also matters whether the stillness is inside or out.

And with all the tender dew condensed on stale
doubts
And the appealing certainty of entropy and its
lost whereabouts
Reflecting tall visions, slowly dissolving the
mind.
This life is a mountain hanging by a thread,
you'll find
As it keeps on hanging in stillness for certain;
And the thought of moving the mountain is not
one you'll entertain.
As stillness is calming, as you fear the thread
can only take so much,
And the milestones and the treacherous paths
are hostile to touch;
And a step will get you started and keep on
going you will
And you shall move the planted mountain and
yet stay still.

The Heart

It's alright, the heart doesn't know
So long as it beats, it'll want some more
Once you settle down, it'll yearn for a new place to go
And of course I know, the story has been told before.

When you look on from a distance, trying to get in
The door has been shut, and it's a cold night;
And you wonder if yearning is a sin
And of course I know; the heart sees everything in this light.

If you think you'll never make it, you're not alone;
Hearing whispers of rumoured tales of a utopia far away
And you bought the tickets for your heart is not made of stone
And of course I know, my heart too dreamt of that one day.

And the time wasted in the limbo, going round and round,
You've lagged behind, and many steps are overdue:
But it is when you stopped walking you have found
That of course you know, everyone has a heart just like you.

Ships of Stone

Ships of stone
In the waters of your eyes
Flesh and bone
In the yearnings of skies
Wishes of wizards
In illegible blueprints
Medley of blizzards
In organized stints
And then the question is asked
And I am afraid I do not know yet.

Words of no meanings
In a misplaced letter
Adding of unscheduled winnings
In a bid to get better
Curtailing of levelling
In a serrated plain
Oxidation of revelling
In a truncated disdain
And then the question is asked
And I am afraid I do not know yet.

And then the world is seen
And it doesn't make it any better
And the hearts and minds are keen
But the former is cautioned by the latter
And we look at each other, helpless,
Wondering what the other might think
Aboard that stone ship, ashore and hapless
We will thrive and we will sink -
And we're all lost, till we find our way,
Whichever road to wherever we call home.
And we collect flowers and thorns that lay
In the wake of our divergent steps set in
chrome.
And for the missions we are tasked
We may win them with fate, but lose the bet
And for the question that is asked
I have found out, but I cannot tell you yet.

Sun, Earth And Water

How they learned to create poetry with sun, earth and water,
And fulfill and complete a society, churning days into nights –
How they learned to watch something grow like their son or daughter
And shape it into beauty, calming not just to the sights.
How they learned to sweat and bleed into the ground
And grow gold and still walk on their feet,
How they learned to always look for what needs to be found
And make sure the cycle is complete.
How they learned what works after tribulations of trial and error
And shared with the world the fruit.
How they learned to carry on when the world isn't fairer
And spend the nights living by the truth.

How they learned to endure the wrath of nature
And understand for it is the same force that gives life.
How they learned to leave their signature
And create generations looked up to when tragedies are rife.
How they learned to teach hard work can still create beauty,
And stay in touch with the old ways in new times.
How they learned to let temptations by and devote to their duty
And return back simply, becoming their poetry's rhymes.

Dark Clouds

When the dark clouds come roll by
Will I have had my time to weep?
Just as the sound of the alarm rings by
Will I have had just enough sleep?
And when it's my time to go by
Will you still be mine to keep?

When I have your glass full
I still flirt with the brim,
I still go the extra mile
Along the edge of the stream,
Forgetting what I came to find
On a calculated whim.

Just as the night falls
I start laying the bricks
Building a strong and tall wall
Fooled by no tricks –
Fooled just by myself anticipating
Something thrown that sticks.

I go and get my tools

As it begins to rain;
For someone's stair
I build an equivalent mountain:
Steep, with no vantage
Has it all gone to vain?

Can you teach me to look over
When my heart starts beating fast?
Can you convince me I'm wrong
When I know I will end up last?
Will you still hold my hand
When the sunny days have gone past?

Let Go

The air is fresh, and cold
And it is a quiet night;
With all the triumphs wasted on being bold
And all the principles abandoned for being right
You have held on.

With the world spinning
And falling accomplice to the maddening misbelief;
With all the determination wasted on winning
And all the faith lost for grief
You have held on.

Chance after chance, day after day
Retracing the dots, with a lesson yet to learn;
With all the words wasted on what you couldn't say
And all the hope strangled on being stubborn
You have held on.

And at the end, you will realize

That it is all happening
And you are gentle and okay.
And all your worries will turn to ashes
Disfiguring into the cold air
As it leaves your tired lungs
As you let go.

Here To Stay

As you go around in circles and wonder what's the point,
As you try your hardest and still fear you'll disappoint;
The world, with its eyes, is here to stay
And so are you.
As you lend a hand to a weight heavier than you can pull,
As you give yet another gift to someone with their bag full;
The world, with its needs, is here to stay
And so are you.
As you give space only to be pushed into a corner,
As you lend a shoulder only to be left a loner;
The world, with its indulgence, is here to stay
And so are you.
As you only learn with sore hands to let go
As you only learn with a broken heart to know
You will drown but the world is buoyant
You only learn going around in circles about the point.

The mist hangs over, inundating
Hugging all life in a nurturing embrace;
"I bring nectar from the skies, celebrating,
For it is your time to grow now, in my grace."

Voices and Rhymes

Thus the mountain shall stand tall
And cradle new life in its lap
And thus the water shall fall
Off the height into a limitless tap –
Voices that dissolved others
Voices that wield mountains to amplify
Voices that transcend through the water which mothers
Voices that smash into barriers just to multiply
Voices that have taught a tongue
To the teething infants
Voices that have passed through lung to lung
Voices that made poets and militants
And everything in between –
They shall prevail through the halls of life
To be ever-heard and ever-seen
To be the bandage and to be the knife
To be one to all and all to one.
The water shall not ask for direction
Nor shall the light –
The waves shall not wait for anyone

Nor shall the blight.
Humble, on the sand
At Sun's bathing time
Ponders with a pen in hand
Of a perpetual rhyme –
A rhyme that shall invoke the immortal voices
Or just become them.
A rhyme strict, but offering choices
Flowering out of its stem.
A rhyme flowering, like fountains,
Mothered by the boundless waters
Cradled in the lap of fatherly mountains
A rhyme, growing, like daughters
Of a lost breed –
Neighbouring a lonely monolith,
As the voices pass by, ricochet, and succeed
The rhyme hopes one day to become one with.

Antiquity

Catapult a gaze, as far as the eye can see,
Overriding emotions with the help of curiosity,
Holding onto things world labelled as obsolete
It'll be your one and only while it's the world's
antiquity.

Walk barefoot on the grass with a fresh sun
taking a peek
As the birds alarm the world with their beaks,
And do not resist and be taken by the breeze
And that's one way you can fly with grounded
feet.

Help something grow just because you can
Be true to yourself even if no one will
understand
We all run amuck and go to sleep, and look for
tranquility,
And you do not know the extent of your ability.

Protect that little part of you that still cares

Even if they make it feel like running backwards
up the stairs.
Loving is easy and kindness is natural
proclivity:
Make them your own while the world turns
them into antiquity.

Wilderness

Lost in the wilderness by imposed deception
You saw ever since it started conspiring,
You held on a while longer to allow the
interception
By something just dreaming of aspiring,
Held the hands of the ones who stumbled
And have learned to walk since:
Made sure the shade was on for when it
rumbles
For ones who just want to rinse
Their hands off of the linear decree
Of the infectious light you radiate,
Lost in their own dark wilderness to a degree
That the fresh air has begun to suffocate
And yet they'd kill for it at the same time.
Ignoring the elephant in the room
As if materialisation of such a thing is a crime.
Sweeping off your prints off your stairs with a
broom
They used to climb, to look down on you.
More remarkable if broken than perfect

As the world unleashes on cue
Eulogies to the weathered statues that no
longer stand erect.
You dig deep, deeper into the lightless mine
Finding treasures whose values don't match up,
You wait patiently at the finish line
For the rest of the lost world to catch up.

Rapid and Slow

At times, it feels so still
And in a blink, inundated with metamorphosis.
Dead roses on layered limestone,
Sky-poking mountains growing from the
ground –
Slowly and slowly,
In perspective, so rapidly
Milestones of history
Compasses of the future
Chants of the beds below
And bringing down messages from up above –
Amalgamating into ever-running waterfalls
With a perpetual song,
Washing the nestling world in its haze
As it grows
Slowly, and slowly,
In perspective, so rapidly
And who are we to say,
Who are we to count?
Conducted by the composer
We follow the tempo

And we play our parts, and then go,
And we think,
We had all the time in the world
Yet, it was not enough.

A Good Word (House of Mirrors)

What do you know of sacrifice?
What do you know of loneliness,
What do you know of pain?
What do you know of heartbreak,
What do you know of regret?
You can never know it all
For each and every one of us;
But you can know of compromise,
You can know of giving company
You can know of care
You can know of love
And you can know of hope –
For a bad word reverberates
Worsening, before being lost –
And we are all pools of water
Mirroring our own insides
To the other mirrors we see –
Like calming the ripples
Or causing them –
For a good word echoes
And is reflected, in this funny house of mirrors
And it is never lost.

Pull The Cord

Grand vessels, rendering you a mere passenger
Transformative news, rendering you a mere messenger
And the road is long, and no one knows where or if it ends
And you have traversed a part of it once, you know these bends
And you have heard rumours of what is to come
And you have heeded to them, while you disregarded some
And you have filtered through your immaculate sieve
What you have heard and seen, still you are not sure what to believe -
And we're in the same boat together,
Passengers with a crumpled ticket each
With the destination scribbled in illegible writing, and the timings which
Are not from the clocks we know and use
And it left you confused and me obtuse.

So, we'll sit and see, savour in the funny feeling in the stomach
Each time the car speeds; and leave it all to fate and luck
And still make plans, while we still can
Leaving room for rain for when it doesn't go according to plan.
And we'll sit in this bus, and take in the show through the glass screens
We call windows, and fall in awe of the blues and greens
And while we have each other, we have everything we can afford
We'll arrive at our destination some time; we don't have to pull the cord.

Time And Waves

Well, it takes away everything fragile you build.
It also possesses an alibi.
It comes vigorously, and it killed
Whatever is left to die.

These waves demolish all the castles of sand
And exhibit their rage.
It comes with nothing in hand
But takes away everything in its limitless cage.

The waves come and touch my feet.
And they look so exquisite.
Because a lamp does a spark lit
Also the raging blazes of the hells beneath.

Till posterity, time and waves shall come and go.
Compromising nothing, pushing the shore...

Blue

It was all blue, and cold
Once when it was very old
And with hovering ominous smoke
And gentle sounds in a deceptive cloak
Slowly and slowly, give away;
And yet it takes nothing to sway
The minds surrounded by astounding beauty
Deserving to be worshipped as if it were the duty
And it is vast, spanning distances
Inducing imitated instances
Where the selves are caressingly peeled away
As some notice the shrunken sun on a setting day,
So oblivious, but to sing the praises, where does one start
As all of it stems from it, everything is a part –
For there is the sun
And we are the rays
For there is the ocean
And we are the drops

For there is the Earth
And we are life...

Helpless, at the feet of a sleeping giant, we stay
And slowly and slowly, give away
As our home is set on fire and our possessions drowned
And we sit pretty on our thrones, still crowned
With ashes and rusted mold
Which has found its home in something that old;
And we go on, and go on, come what may
And slowly and slowly, give away
As the story has already been told
As we grow feeding on ashes into a rusty mold.

What Have You...

And what have you seen
Through your tired eyes? –
A grain of sand carried by an ant
And the blue whale in the ever-stretching oceans
And the stars in the unfathomably boundless universe –
And what you see is your world
Full of people, things and emotions,
But what have you really seen?

And what have you touched
With your weak hands? –
The hand of a friend holding on to you,
The hand of a lover you finally let go,
The delicate new life looking up to you –
And what you touch is your world
Full of life, lifeless things and sometimes something in between,
But what have you really touched?

And what have you felt
With your aching heart? –
The joy of being loved
The sorrow of being alone and not enough
And the bittersweet taste you can't quite pinpoint sometimes,
And what you feel is your world
Full of happiness, pain and everything in between and around,
But what have you really felt?

And with your tired eyes and weak hands and aching heart
You tether your miniscule world and then tear it apart;
You climb the ladder and then fall down,
You hide your head in shame and then wear a crown.
And a glance at the wide world, outside looking in
Reveals how you are felt, touched and seen
And then you know that you aren't alone and are enough,

And you are the world, and everything that makes it up.

Lion Heart

She just stands there,
Handed the wrong end of fair,
And there is no time for argument,
Yet showing no signs of disappointment
She just stands there
As they wonder whether she's got a heart
Or she knew it all from the start
Or has it just turned to stone
After all this time being all alone?
All she's left to give is her love
As she's run out of her riches now,
Or so does she think.
She opens up her arms without a blink
As she just stands there.

And of course they don't know her at all,
She goes alone to bed as nights fall.
Her eyes stay wide open all night
Leakproof, like her eyes have been shut tight,
As she prays to the Almighty for a heart of a
lion -

Fearless, strong, and the heroine of a scion;
And the sunlight shatters her chance at a dream every dawn
Yet she dares to try each night until the darkness is gone.
And they see her as she goes about her day without a care
As they hand her the wrong end of fair
And then spew out pity and wonder again
Has she gone numb from all the pain?
And the cycle then repeats
As the world again cheats
Her as she longs for a lion heart at night
To be brave enough to fight her plight
And she just stands there as the world moves on,
All the familiar faces are long gone;
All she sees are sheep everywhere
As she just stands there,
Not realizing hearts come in cages but they are free
And she's braver than a lion could ever be.

The Sun Is Working Overtime

Puzzled, the King sank into his throne,
Mourning what he lost while he was winning in his prime,
All the realms of men singing his name,
He wonders whether his glory was ever worth a dime.

We scratch our heads at the crossroads,
When the cars stop, we look around to follow the line.
It is a sweet compromise, you see?
We all have to reach somewhere to sell our skill and time, in time.

We console ourselves by over-telling fables,
Dreaming of being kings and queens in a happy song's rhyme.
The puzzled King is jealous, and it is an unfamiliar feeling,
Ruler of the free people trapped in his golden throne and grandiose palace in this mime.

Roses, the smell and the thorns, red and white,
Are all roses after all; is thinking otherwise a crime?
Get your hand off of your head, and stop complaining,
This beautiful evening, the sun is working overtime.

My Friend

Why are you lost, my friend?
Is it that you haven't found what you were looking for
Or have simply stumbled into an unending end?
Or is it that you have seen enough of the war
And you are clad in impenetrable armour, strayed from the battlefield
Fighting for yourself still, in a maze you yourself have set?
Or is it that you have tried a million ways to yield
But you end up meaning that word to give up, rather than to get?

Why are you angry, my friend?
Is it that you carry around a back-breaking load
Of tools obsolete and useless that only you can understand?
Or is it that you have realized that you have undersold
Your time and strength and heart and soul?

Anger is a coward's blunt tool
And until now you have played the hero's role -
Beware, for it is something that turns the smartest into a fool.

Are you okay, my friend?
Is it that you have tried desperately holding on to the past
And hastily preparing for a future that you can't comprehend?
And realized you forgot to live, you forgot to live at last:
It is not the end, or the battlefield or the weight
For it could be the start, the home, the lifting hand
As you will get there someday, you won't be late -
And if you understand that, you are okay, my friend.

Carry On

Stand tall even with weak knees
Even when heights once conquered
Seem out of reach,
Even when the worlds you once carried
With ease,
Now break your back,
Even when solved mysteries
Start appearing strange, out of some daydream
Once forgotten, but with a new lease
On hope, you carry on.

Lend a hand even with a betrayed arm,
Even when you take a chance
That can't be predicted by reading your palm,
Even when you've learned the lesson
And have been cautioned by the alarm,
Even when you have once reached out in vain
For something that just didn't heed your
terrible charm,
Even when you underestimate your insurance
in faith

That doesn't just cater to the one animal, but
the entire farm -
You learn to carry on.

You Have Lived

When you push the limits
To see how far you can go,
When you count the minutes
To the start of the show,
When you give it your all
At the end of the day,
When you answer the final call
And somehow find a way,
When you precisely skate the overlapping edges
Of futility and moments of brilliance
To find a reason to try just once more, among patches
Of temptations and resilience
When you find a sparkle of hope
In the dark night
And find the strength to cope
At the loss of sight
You have lived.

They are deceiving little things, the limits

They only exist at your will.
They are no more than gimmicks
Self-designed to keep yourself still;
When you stop seeing the thorns and only see the road,
When you calibrate yourself and look outside
And not let it adulterate your abode
As you are saturated inside;
When you walk on with circled persistence
And an elevated set of eyes, heart and mind,
You reject the path of least resistance
As even if you were blind
You'd find the beauty, as you see
Pain as the fuel of strength,
Being limited as a chance to break free.
As you stop worrying about the road and its length
As now you know limits exist only if you think they do.
And ignorance is bliss as they say, it won't let anything grow.
And the world is beautiful, it is true,
It only takes seeing to know.

And then you'll realize you only thought you had lived.

We'd Know

Well, it is a long road,
And there are places we have to go:
For wherever we choose to root our abode
We'd hope we're happy and we remain so.

Well, somewhere along this crooked path
We'll fall in doubt and come to a halt:
For when something doesn't add up in the math
We'd hope we'd be wise enough to absorb the fault.

Well, for everything we hear and see
And for all the words we hold in between:
For compensating each breath to release free
We'd hope we're heard and seen.

Well, we know there'll be highs and lows
And we'll stay level through them, we'll have learned:
For we know we'll eventually slow down, that's how it goes

We'd hope we're content with what we've
earned.

Well, when we feel all the debts have been paid
Or so has the time come to meet the sea:
For everything that we leave behind and have
laid
We'd know we had found love, you and me.

About The Author

KAP 5 is the pen name of Krunal Patel, an author from India, residing in Canada. He started out writing poems at a really young age, and then extrapolated into writing novels and short stories. In December 2024, he published his first book, Shrouded Skies, a collection of his poems. He works in healthcare.

www.ingramcontent.com/pod-product-compliance
Lightning Source LLC
Chambersburg PA
CBHW061002050726
47592CB00003B/1309

* 9 7 8 1 0 6 9 2 3 0 0 0 3 *